# Contents

# Early life

Wolfgang Amadeus Mozart was born in Salzburg, Austria, on 27 January 1756. When he was three years old he liked to stand on a chair and sing songs for his mother, father and sister.

Mozart watched his big sister Nannerl play the **clavier**. He wanted to learn too. His father began teaching him to play when he was four years old.

# A talented child

When Mozart was five, he began to make up his own music. This is called **composing**. Mozart could also play the **clavier**, violin and organ when he was six.

Mozart did not go to school. His father taught him at home. He liked Maths and Music best. He wrote sums on blackboards on the walls of his house.

# Travel

When Mozart was seven he and Nannerl went on a long **tour** of Europe with their father. They played music to kings and queens and other important people.

Mozart was very ill while he was away from home. He caught **typhoid** and **smallpox**. These illnesses made him a weak child.

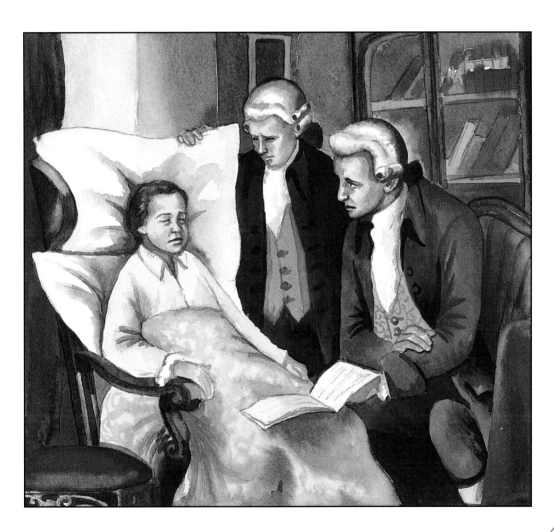

# Making music

At the age of nine, Mozart wrote his first **symphony** for a whole **orchestra**. He also learnt how to **conduct** an orchestra.

As he grew up, Mozart earned money by **composing** and playing music for rich and important people. These people were called **patrons**.

# Opera

When Mozart was 25, he went to live in Vienna, Austria. There he met and married a woman called Constanze. Their son, Franz, grew up to be a **composer** as well.

Mozart composed a lot of famous music in Vienna. He liked writing **opera** best. One of his operas is called *The Magic Flute*.

# Debt

Mozart was paid money for his music. He and Constanze had their own house and servants. But they were always in **debt** because Mozart did not earn enough money.

Mozart died on 5 December 1791. He was only 35 years old. Many people thought Mozart was the greatest musical **composer** in the world.

# Paintings

There are many ways in which we can find out about Mozart. We can look at paintings of him. Here is a painting of him when he was six.

# House

You can visit the house in Salzburg where Mozart was born. Now it is a museum. In the house, you can see the **clavier** Mozart used to play.

# Letters

Mozart wrote many letters to his family and his friends when he was travelling. Here is a letter that he wrote to his wife in the year he died.

Many things were written about Mozart during his life. This is a **leaflet** advertising his **opera** *Don Giovanni*.

# Music

Here is a **manuscript** written by Mozart when he was eleven. It shows how Mozart wrote his music on the page. It also shows how he crossed it out to make changes.

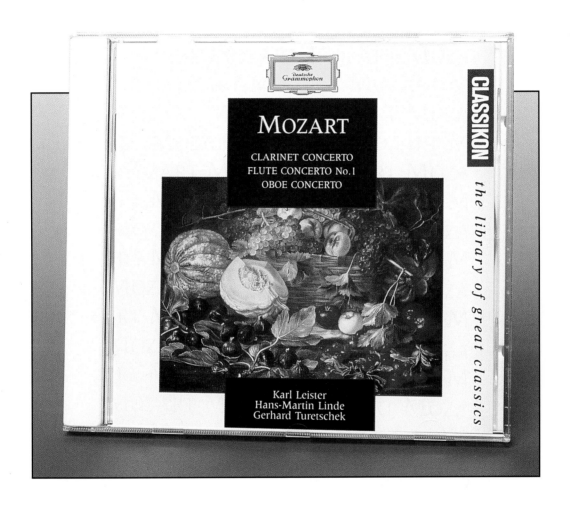

Mozart's music is still played at **concerts** all over the world. You can listen to his music on a CD or on the radio.

# Remembering Mozart

Mozart and his music are as popular as ever. This film about his life was made in 1984. The film is called *Amadeus*.

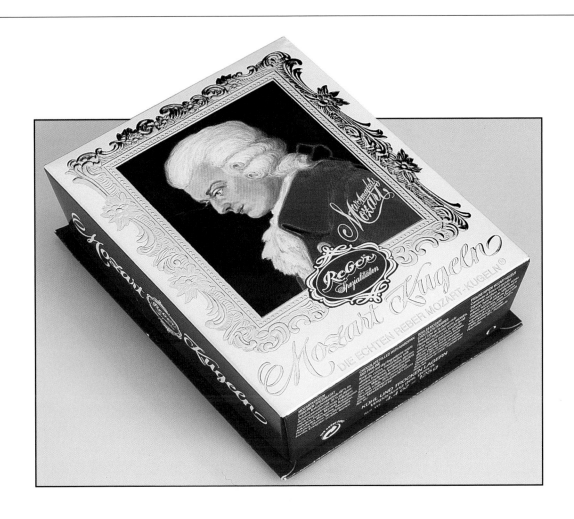

These chocolate balls are named after
Mozart. You can buy them in special sweet
shops all over the world. This shows how
popular Mozart still is.

# Glossary

This glossary explains difficult words, and helps you to say words which may be hard to say.

**clavier** keyboard instrument. A piano is a clavier. You say *klav-ee-ay*.

**compose** make up music

**concert** public show by musicians or singers. You say *kon-sert*.

**conduct** help an orchestra to play music in time

**debt** having no money. You say *det*.

**leaflet** printed sheet of paper with information on it

**manuscript** music written by hand. You say *man-you-script*.

**opera** play full of songs

**orchestra** large group of musicians who play their different musical instruments together. You say *or-kes-tra*.

**patron** someone who gives money or support to a person or group. You say *pay-tron*.

**smallpox** bad illness which gives you fever and a rash

**symphony** long piece of music (in three or four parts) for many musical instruments. You say *sim-fun-ee*.

**tour** long journey to different countries. You say *taw*.

**typhoid** bad illness which gives you fever and spots. You say *tie-foyd*.

# Index